Love With No Conditions

A Collection of True Stories

Love With No Conditions

A Collection of True Stories

by

Bren Claborn
Amber Galloway
Beverly Hearn
Jann Kisseberth
Crystal Koch
Jerry Koch
Terri Lerner
Tiffany Lobo
Charlie Lombard
Judi Manis
Joel Mizell
Geneva Norwood
Dianne Price
Katie Roof
Terri Schneberger
Mary Sutter
Kim Vizza
Carol Ward

Love With No Conditions
Copyright © 2015 by Empyrion Publishing

ISBN: 978-0692584590

Empyrion Publishing
PO Box 784327
Winter Garden, FL
Info@EmpyrionPublishing.com

Unless otherwise noted, all Scripture quotations are from the King James Version.

New Living Translation is indicated as NLT.

Printed in the United States of America

Forward

by
Rick Manis

We all deal with this fallen world, and we are all hit by its adverse conditions. However, God has a way of filling our hearts with the power of love that is greater than anything in this world. This inner power is the secret to a heaven on earth experience.

In *Love with No Conditions*, Judi did not necessarily seek out the most earth-shattering, wildest testimonies. Instead, she invited everyday people to share an example of their experience with the love and goodness of God. You will relate to many of them as they share about the God who is very personal to all of us, and who loves us and cares for us in the middle of our very different situations.

God could be defined as the love that has no conditions. It's the love that nobody has to qualify for. It's the love that has no boundaries, and nothing is too big or too small for God. This is a collection of love stories, a collection of gratitude expressed from thankful hearts.

Love with No Conditions paints a corporate expression of the God who loves and believes in you. Enjoy.

Table of Contents

Introduction

I have had the unique opportunity to accompany my husband as he travels and encourages people in churches, home groups and various organizations with the good news of God's unconditional love and grace. As a result, I've had the privilege of meeting a myriad of people from all walks of life whose lives have been transformed by an awareness of God's forgiveness, favor, and delight in them. Their stories have touched me deeply.

In recent years there seems to me to be a revolution of increased understanding of the gospel of Jesus Christ sweeping the body of Christ. The fear that embracing grace will give people a license to sin is diminishing. Instead people are experiencing the depth of love that God has for them personally and they are being empowered to walk out of addictions, heartbreak, sickness, grief, poverty and even just the mundane stresses of life. It didn't appear to make logical sense that being loved would actually enable us to behave differently, love better, and prosper in life. Nevertheless, we are seeing it to be true with ever-increasing clarity.

One day while I was sitting in a service I had the idea of compiling a number of these stories together which illustrate how the revelation of God's unconditional love is making a difference in people's lives. This awareness comes in unique ways and manifests in various forms. Every issue of life has an answer in Jesus Christ.

In this book you won't find formulas to follow, but hopefully you will find encouragement in hearing how others with similar concerns or circumstances as you were able not only to overcome, but to prosper. Each individual has voluntarily contributed to this book with the sole purpose of sharing what they have experienced in the hopes of helping someone else.

Only the Holy Spirit can open our eyes to revelation, but we hope our testimonies will provide a means for the Holy Spirit to reveal and minister life into whatever you are currently walking through. May you be blessed and encouraged as you read these pages.

Judi Manis

His Pursuit

As a child I grew up in a very legalistic home with a father who was a preacher, and a very discontented and disconnected mother. The resulting neglect led to a constant pursuit of attention and approval on my part. I lived a life that was less than pleasing to my parents, culminating with a pregnancy at the age of fourteen, a forced marriage, having three children by the age of eighteen, and ultimately a divorce. Many things followed that downward spiral of my floundering childhood and young adult life, but there is not enough time here to tell of them all. After a second marriage to another much older and extremely abusive man, who passed away after eighteen years of marriage, I was left in so many pieces that I just didn't see much hope of a future. The religious upbringing that I had constantly condemned me for all the failures in my life.

So, the short of a very long story begins with my Father coming to my rescue to show me what a father really is and also what a lover and husband could be in His kingdom. God knew that because of the lack of a father's involvement in my life, and the difficulties I had experienced in marriage, it would take another kind of man to show me what it truly meant to be a father and husband, so he answered my longing cry by doing just that. I met the most amazing man who showed me God's love in a tangible way. I was very skeptical at first, of course, but I began to yield to this romancing of my Father through this man. It truly was the most awesome grace one could experience. I married him and my life hasn't been the same since. I have truly experienced, and do experience, heaven on earth every single day.

This expression of my Father's love for me opened the door for me to receive the truth of the meaning of His grace, where all that I had previously been condemned by could be replaced by His words of acceptance and unconditional love. I heard this true message of grace through one particular ministry, and the Holy Spirit has been expanding my understanding of God's grace and love ever since, which has resulted in the renewing of my mind and freedom from all those years of condemnation. I'm so grateful to my Daddy for his unfailing love!

Kimberly Vizza
Lakeland, Florida

A Change In My Prayers

I was raised in church and my husband and I spent years leading a youth ministry in our local church. I've always had a desire to live a life that would be pleasing to God. However, I never felt that I quite measured up to God's expectations.

In the evenings, I would pray to God before I went to sleep, asking Him to forgive me of how I had fallen short that day. Every day there would be numerous examples of how I had let Him down. From mistakes that I made to heart attitudes that weren't quite right to the lackluster love I seemed to feel towards the Lord, I felt I was a continual disappointment to Him. If only I would try harder...but it seemed the harder I tried, the more I failed. I didn't realize that my relationship with the Lord was mostly focused on me and my behaviors rather than on Him and His finished work on the Cross. No wonder it felt lackluster.

Unwittingly, I was using condemnation as a way to try to control my behavior and make myself more acceptable to God. There was never a sense of peace or rest, just an unending treadmill of trying to do better. Sometimes I felt good about myself if I compared myself to someone else and sometimes I felt bad about myself, depending on who I was comparing myself to.

When I began to hear and understand the grace of God and the finished work of the Cross, I was able to get off the treadmill and relax. The focus of my relationship with the Lord began to be where it was supposed to have been all along...on Him rather than on me.

I noticed my prayers began to change. In the evenings before I went to sleep, I found myself thanking God for His numerous blessings on my life. Even in difficult circumstances, I would thank Him for never leaving me or forsaking me. I had a real sense that He was for me, not against me...and as result, I was able to rest. I am grateful for this change in my perspective in my relationship with God. It has touched every area of my life including my relationships with my family and friends. Because I am no longer focused on myself and am so much more aware of how pleased and loving God is towards me, I am able to see and appreciate the good all around me every day, both in people and in situations.

As told by Mary Sutter
Claremore, Oklahoma

Formed In Utter Seclusion

My husband and I walked the long journey of infertility for eleven years. I would start each month with anticipation that this would be the month that I would get pregnant. I was injecting fertility medication throughout the day to boost my system. I was also at the doctor's office at least ten times a month. Each month my body would not respond to the medication and each month my period would come and bring with it my broken, devastated, disappointed heart. I would cry it all out, call my doctor and we would start again with a new regimen of medicine and maybe another invasive, painful test or two to try to find out what was wrong.

Despite these outward circumstances, over the years I'd had one confirmation after another that I would have a child from my womb, so we continued with infertility treatments. We were so full of faith that we decorated the nursery. We painted the walls, customized the furniture and I even sewed the bedding for the crib and cradle, but the years would click by and our circumstances remained the same.

What did not remain the same was my relationship with Jesus. When I could not stand, He would hold me up. When my disappointment was too great to take another minute, I would curl up under His strong arms, hide from the world and let Him hold me and heal me. When friends and family would conceive and have children, He would hold my heart while I would experience sincere joy for them, but gut-wrenching pain for me and my empty womb and empty arms. During this long season I experienced the true deep love of God. I did not understand what He was doing but I praised Him and trusted Him and was honest with Him. I told Him I was mad at Him and He said He knew and that it was okay.

One day, during a service at my church, my pastor said, "Tiffany, when you walked in and I met you, the Lord started speaking to me about a word for you. I went and prayed a little bit and this is what the Lord says. You've been asking, you've been asking for a word from God; an answer from God, a directive from God. And here is the word that God has for you about this word, about this directive, about this answer. The word is 'YES. YES.' The Lord says, 'I CAN and I WILL.' He said you can stop asking me. That it's

10

already done. You can begin to rejoice because it's already done. The Lord also comes to encourage you in this way. He comes to say, 'This is more than you know. More than you're experiencing. This is more than just a pat on the back. This is something the Lord is saying to encourage you.' He says, 'I love you and you are very precious to me. I want to reassure you that I am in charge. That I AM the sovereign ruler of the universe. That you have a destiny in me and I will not be stopped. You've never said anything to me that I haven't heard. You've never prayed a prayer that I've not noted. You've never sung a song in worship that hasn't caught my ear. Your time with me is precious to me.' The Lord says, 'Talk to me. The ones who get are the ones who ask. The ones who are willing to receive are the ones I bless. Talk to me, I'll answer you again and again and again and again.'"

As you can imagine, my hope sprung up. It's already done?! I can stop asking?! Well, then I must be going to get pregnant any minute. In fact, I am probably pregnant right now! YAHOO!

PAUSE…Don't miss the second part of the message. It is a love letter to me. I am crying right now reading how much Jesus loves me and took the time to make sure I knew that He is truly in charge and truly in love with me.

PLAY…I did not get pregnant. I have never been pregnant. I don't understand how all of this works, but this is when my story really starts to get good.

Our stopping point came in the summer of 2008. I had run the course, an eleven year, 132 month, course. I was exhausted. There wasn't another test to do, another treatment to try. It was truly the end of the medical journey. After I cried and prayed and for the millionth time wondered where my "YES" was, my husband agreed that we could begin looking into adoption.

On December 7, 2008 our adoption profile went active with our American Adoption's website and we were officially in the queue to be chosen as parents. We were the last family on the website – 176th. Eleven days later on December 18th at 4:30pm our phone rang and my husband, Zemanel, answered it. He came to find me and said it was a social worker with our adoption agency.

We put her on speaker and in the next few minutes our lives hit warp speed. She said there was a baby being born that night and we needed to be prepared to go the next day. When we hung up the phone we were so happy and shocked and excited. We could feel the electricity in the room. I think it was the Holy Spirit jumping up and down with us.

The typical protocol is the birth mother chooses an adoptive family months before the baby is born and during this time she will interview you and then you prepare for the baby to come. Our call came in eleven days. We'd had eleven years of infertility and then God gave us our baby in eleven days.

Izzy's birth mother shared with us how she did not even know that she was pregnant. She'd had her regular cycle all these months and had gone to the doctor only two weeks prior for back pain when he told her she was eight and a half months pregnant! This all happened as the US economy was taking a nosedive and they could not afford to have a third child. She asked a lifelong girlfriend to help her investigate and make an adoption plan. They came across our adoption agency on the internet and were immediately drawn to our profile. Her friend works in real estate and so she liked that we did too. Izzy's birth mother really wanted her baby to grow up in a

Christian home and our profile was filled with Jesus and how important our relationship with Him is to us.

Usually when a birth mother contacts American Adoptions, they will send her the profile of about ten potential parents for her to choose from. In our case, Izzy's birth mother called them and just wanted us. The funny thing is that when they sent out her packet, the agency just sent out their standard ten profiles and ours was not even in the bunch. She called back right way and explained that she REALLY wanted us and that she did not need to look at any other profiles. The adoption agency, of course, apologized for the mix-up and called us right away. Our match was made!

Izzy's birth mother told us that she felt God's hand in our meeting. She said that because she did not know she was pregnant and because her labor pain and childbirth felt like a "mosquito bite," that she had not bonded with the baby. She sincerely felt like the baby was truly ours and that God had used her to give us a child. I can't tell you how overwhelming this is; how loved I feel even to this very moment. What a divine orchestration our loving Father conducted for us.

One of the sweetest and most profound revelations we've had was that because Izzy's birth mother did not know she was pregnant, we realized the Lord had been hiding Izzy in secret for us. Only God knew she existed for those eight and a half months. Many years ago as I really started to understand how much God loved me, it was Psalm 139 that revealed to me the depths of how much God knew me and wanted me. During my infertility I held onto these promises like a life raft. Now, looking at this scripture, with my hidden Izzy in mind, it is too wonderful to realize that she was "being formed in utter seclusion," safe in His care until He delivered her to me.

Psalms 139:13-16: *You made all the delicate, inner parts of my body and knit them together in my mother's womb. Thank you for making me so*

wonderfully complex! It is amazing to think about. Your workmanship is marvelous – and how well I know it. You were there while I was being formed in utter seclusion! You saw me before I was born and scheduled each day of my life before I began to breathe. Every day was recorded in your Book. (NLT)

It did not matter at all that she was not born of my body. She was the Lord's child and He was putting her in my care. What a magnificent honor. As Mary and Joseph were chosen to take care of Jesus, Zemanel and I were chosen to take care of Izzy.

Tiffany Lobo
Author of "Big Good God and Little Busy Izzy"
Winter Garden, Florida

God's Love Is Never Failing

I remember the day I accepted God as my Lord and Savior. It was in a little tiny Baptist church in Lawton, Oklahoma. I was seven years old and that decision was so incredibly emotional. I felt God tugging at my heart and I responded. At seven years old, the words that resonated with me then and now is "God is Love."

However, much of the teaching I received did not demonstrate this all the time. I was told that listening to rock n' roll music or going to school dances would send me to hell. So, I began believing that God's love depended on the situation and my obedience or lack thereof. This warped my view of God and his love towards me.

During the fifth grade, I had to have open heart surgery. I had no fear because I knew God was with me. Yet I believed that God had caused this illness for some reason. I didn't know why He would do such a thing. I just figured I was too young to understand it all, so I didn't give it much more thought.

During the eleventh grade, I had to have another surgery due to a cheerleading accident. I tore a muscle in my knee and had to have it replaced. Again, I believed God did this to me for a reason. This time I thought it was God's way of keeping me from becoming too arrogant.

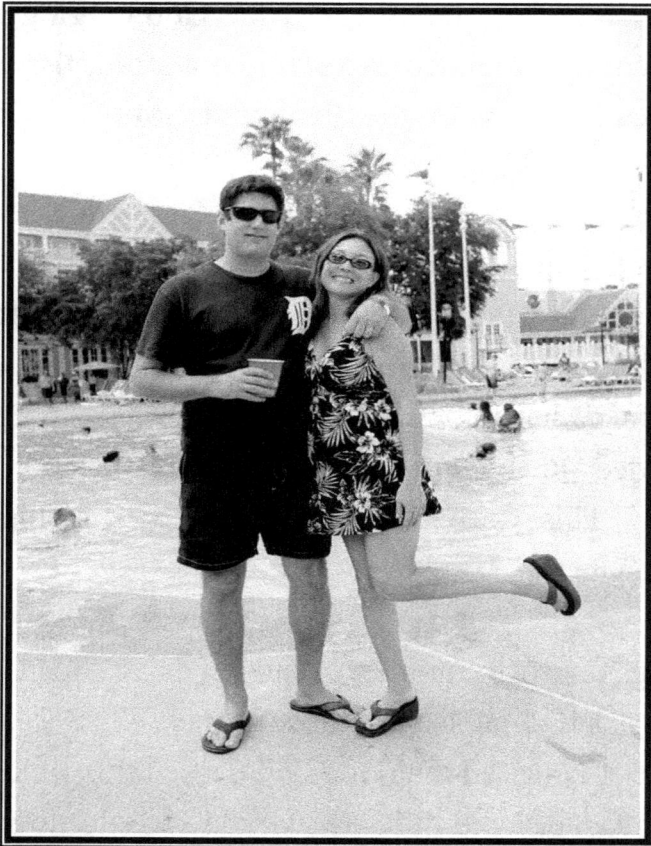

I was in my late 30's when I learned the truth, the solid truth, that God's love is NEVER failing, and that God is the same yesterday, today and tomorrow. His love is constant and doesn't change like the weather or by my actions, thoughts or decisions. ALL my sins are forgiven, which include past, present and future sins.

It was God's love and grace inside me since I was seven years old. Regardless of the warped view I had on God, God's love for me was the same and is still the same, which was and is absolutely awesome!

God did not cause me to have surgeries. He wasn't teaching me a lesson. But, God was and is here with me, always. He will see me though. God turns all of my bad situations into good results.

Jann Kisseberth
Winter Garden, Florida

Freedom From Addiction

I had a sensitivity to God even as a young boy. My family, however, never went to church except on Easter. I realized later in life that my mom and dad were believers but never attended church because of some bad experiences.

At seven years old, while watching Oral Roberts on TV, in tears I asked Jesus into my heart. As a young boy I would often walk to Sunday School. Even years later, as a youth, I still attended church; but after a tour of duty in Vietnam and being honorably discharged from the Marines, I entered college just in time for the "war objectors" and hippy drug days.

It didn't take long in that atmosphere to soon lose my thoughts of God and Jesus. I began experimenting with drugs and got involved in Zen Buddhism. I ended up in the emergency room having my stomach pumped as a result of a drug overdose. Even so, it didn't deter me until I had a supernatural experience with God while on drugs. During that experience, I felt like I was going to die but I just didn't care. God intervened and in a supernatural experience, revealed Himself to me. As a result, I was totally delivered from drugs a short time later.

Within a couple weeks I came into contract with a Jesus-centered ministry for young men on drugs and alcohol. A year later I was working in this ministry helping other young men get free of drugs and to begin a life with Jesus. However, after two years in the ministry, I felt as though my relationship with Jesus was ebbing away. I had become focused on myself and on rules I thought I needed to follow in order to be pleasing to the Father. I would read the bible every day for a designated length of time. I would pray on my knees many times a day because I felt it was better to show humility by praying on my knees. I memorized scripture every day and I fasted often. I did these activities religiously.

I struggled to keep a short sin account, asking God for forgiveness of sinful actions and thoughts almost hourly. Looking back, I think keeping a short sin account was more like the game of "Whac-A-Mole," where you try to hit moles on the head when they pop their heads up through a hole. The more you hit, the better your score. But in the sin game, I was never good enough or fast enough to win. I could never, through repentance, knock the sin down fast enough to have a clean slate. It just wore me out. The more I tried, the worse I got until I began to think that I was crossing an invisible line, edging toward the unforgivable sin of blaspheming the Holy Spirit. I had unknowingly become incarcerated under law and religion.

Those who looked at me from the outside thought I was doing great, but it was only behavior modification. I was doing all the right things outside, but felt horrible on the inside. I was sin conscious 24/7, falling out of bed at night, onto my knees, if I had a sinful dream.

I had no idea that the law is a ministry of death and a ministry of condemnation (2 Corinthians 3). I guess I had missed that in my bible. In the hands of the devil, law and religion would bring me into condemnation, oppression and death. As I began this downward spiral, I couldn't stop it because I didn't even know what was happening to me.

I finally packed up and left the ministry with a girl I would soon marry. I had come to feel that I could no longer live up to God's standards. Within a few years after I got married, I was using drugs and alcohol again. I went back to hanging around the same familiar gang. By now, I thought I had for sure crossed the line and committed the unpardonable sin. I thought that since I was going to hell, I might as well live it up until the end. This kind of deception can happen if you enter into a relationship with law and religion instead of a life-giving relationship with Jesus Christ.

I lived under this curse of fear and death for nineteen years. My marriage eventually ended in divorce. I purchased a large sailboat and cruised throughout the Caribbean trying to forget about God and all my problems. Nevertheless, the drugs, alcohol and decadent lifestyle were about to come to an end. Finding my lifestyle no longer satisfying, I began to think about suicide. I had finally and totally come to the end of myself. However, it was during this time that I began to sense the presence of God again in my life. Somehow, I just felt like He was drawing me back to Him. It was like He had shifted the winds until I came sailing back to Home Port.

I don't really know how to explain it, but I began to know there must be something about our Father, about Jesus, and about His love for me that I had never known or understood before. I was still dealing with guilt, wanting to please Him now more than ever. After all, I felt I had lost my salvation, but He made it clear to me that I was always His son and never lost that privilege and should I have died during those years, I would have been with Him in heaven. This is called Grace!

He began to birth in me a new desire for His presence and a relationship with Him. Again, I supernaturally lost my desire for alcohol and drugs. He then began to lead me to understand the true gospel, the gospel message of Grace that the Apostle Paul taught. It has forever changed my heart and my life.

Jerry Koch
Author of "Jesus At the Helm"
Asheville, North Carolina

A Miracle of Life

My husband left me for my best friend after twelve years together. It took every bit of life out of me. I was so heavily affected by this that I couldn't get out of bed for more than two weeks. The only thing I knew could save me was Jesus.

To be honest I didn't know how to find him in my despair. I called a friend who right away took me to a ladies bible study. It was truly my saving grace. It took me forever to come out of it, but my new friends helped to show me the way to the Lord again. Being so codependent, however, I began a downward spiral of dating the wrong type of men. I was searching feverishly for the one who would fill me. Don't get me wrong, I KNEW I should be letting Jesus fill me, but I was still so broken. My Abba knows me so well; he knew I needed something physical. After being told for more than fifteen years that I was infertile, He blessed me (quite unexpectedly), with a baby girl. My miracle baby – Hunter Grace. She is the most amazing gift in the world and now I have that physical being to hold onto. Ah, my Lord knows me so well. She is now three years old and blesses all those she meets.

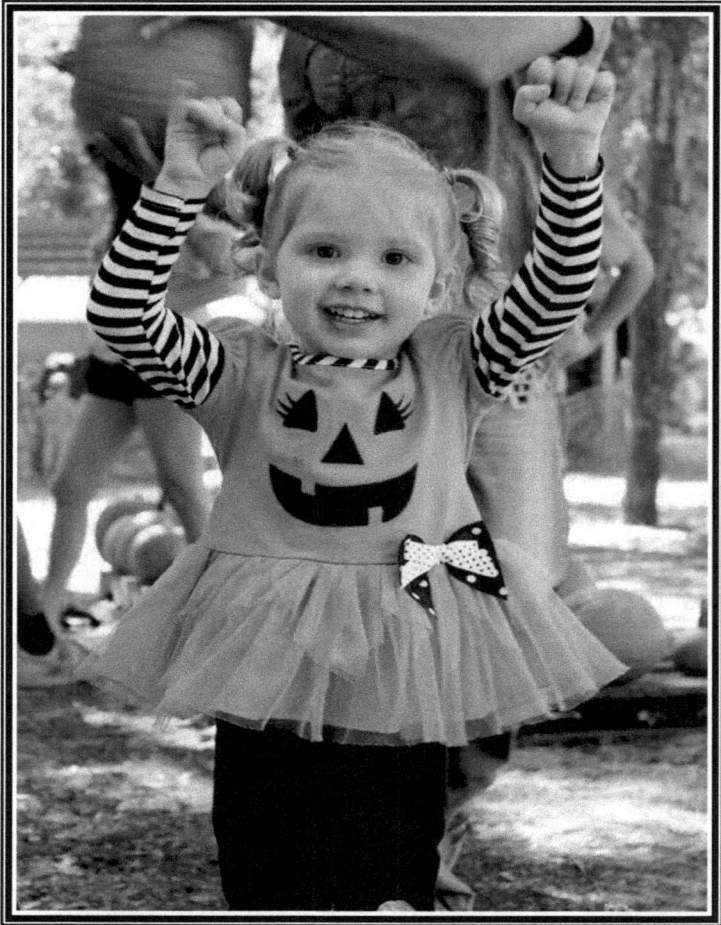

A few months ago she spent a week at my parent's house. They are advocates for Choose Life, and one day their church was holding a little demonstration outside of an abortion clinic. This clinic sits adjacent from a women's center that helps couples who are in a tough spot but don't want to get an abortion. Hunter Grace was with them and she delighted in waving at passersby and singing songs of praise with the other church members. My dad was holding her and a car kept circling the block several times. Finally the gentlemen driving pulled up alongside my father and asked him, "Is this the abortion clinic?" My dad said, "Yes, but you don't want to go there. You want to go across the street. They will help you, and the end result will be just like this beautiful baby." My daughter then waved at him and said, "HI!" The man thanked him and drove across the street. My parents watched to see if they were just going for show, but they didn't come back out. The pregnant woman in the car with him, at one point came out, got her purse and went back in. My parents cried. They knew that Hunter Grace's presence potentially helped save that unborn child's life. Out of all the people there, he spoke to the man holding a precious baby. It was a huge revelation to me that she not only saved me, but she can save others. God gave her to me for a reason. He gave her to the world for a different reason. She is a true miracle.

Terri Lerner
Windermere, Florida

A New Way of Doing School

Thirteen years ago, I was teaching at a Christian school I loved, but kept having ideas of other ways of doing things. One day, my husband said to me, "Hon, you should start a school." To which I replied, "Well you should just open a mall!" I'm a teacher. I did not think I had the ability to start a school. In hindsight, I can see that God spoke to him first. Two years later I began to consider his crazy suggestion.

Things began happening at work and I could tell God was moving me out of my school and comfort zone. Change is not easy for me and I kept asking, "Are your sure God?" After some coaxing by the Lord, I began meeting in homes with friends and parents I knew. The Lord would put people on my heart and I would invite them to join us. Together, we just started dreaming. These people became my "leadership committee." One day, a group of twelve moms and I went to lunch and discussed what they wanted a perfect school to look like. "Terri, why don't you do it?" they asked. This began my year long journey in starting a school, something I knew little to nothing about. Keep in my mind, we did not have a building, not one teacher, and not one dime to start this school with. At this point, it was just a massive brainstorming project.

I would keep a pencil and paper by my bed during this season and the Lord would wake me up and tell me certain things and I would write them down. One thing I felt in particular, was that we seemed to be losing our families. Kids get up, they go to school, they get home at 3:00, then there is homework, extracurricular activities, baths and dinner and "Dad-time" in there somewhere. I really felt we needed to stop the chaos and get our families back. That is how we came up with our name, Family Christian School. That is also why we felt it was crucial to shorten our school days. We do the exact same curriculum as we did during the long school days, we just don't start and stop a lot. This way, the child gets to go home with Mom, tell her about their day, do a little homework, and play. They have time for ball or dance and then Dad comes home. It relaxes the crazy schedule a bit and gives more opportunity for family time and interaction.

We also felt that rote memorization of bible verses in exchange for getting a good grade wasn't the best method for genuine heart understanding of the Word of God. We wanted our kids to really hide the Word of God in their hearts. So, we decided to spend one month on each bible verse rather than just a week. We would also make it a school-wide bible verse so that all grades were studying the same verse. We dissect it every day for the month and teach the full meaning of each verse. This way, when the child or children get to the dinner table, the whole family can talk about it together.

Although the ideas were coming, we really had no way of implementing any of it. At one point, I became very discouraged and honestly felt like the Lord had the wrong person for the job. I got up one morning and said to the Lord, "Unless you hand write me a note or something so specific that I know that I know that I know its from You, I am going to step back and let someone else do this. I did not tell anyone what I had said to the Lord, not even my husband. Within two hours the office of the school I was working at called and said, "Terri, you have flowers." I went to the office and saw a gigantic, funeral-sized, beautiful bouquet of flowers. The card had nothing but a bible verse on it. I ran through the hall yelling, "God sent me flowers!" I had my confirmation. From that point on, I knew without a doubt that I was called and that I would somehow do this seemingly impossible thing.

It got to be summer and I had five teachers. One of the teachers I met with asked me how we were going to get paid. I said, "We are going to trust God." And she said, "Okay." Imagine that? She said okay. Even though she had a job at a very established school, she said, "That make sense to me. Lets do it!"

I would meet with the parents and teachers and say, "Well, I am not sure where we are going to meet." But people kept coming, signing their kids up for our school. Who signs up for a school that doesn't exist? We had no building and a few teachers. Reasonable people don't do this.

We met with church after church, but we could not secure a building. Door after door kept closing. It was July, and we still had no building. School would start in August! One day, I came to talk with the pastor at the church we are now at and he agreed to let us use their facilities. At the time the building was not being used and there was literally nothing but a few chairs in each classroom. In late July, the teachers and their husbands came and we cleaned and painted and hung boards in the classrooms, preparing them for the start of school.

I felt like God had told me that we would start with fifty students in our school. On the first day of school we had a total of forty-seven. I remember telling God, "That is so awesome! You got us about fifty students. Wow! Thank you." Right then, on the first day of school, a family walked in with three children. And we had our fifty. Just like the Lord had said.

About three years after our school had started, a couple of hurricanes came through the area and we were so thankful that nothing really impacted us here. However, one of our dads owns a trucking company and he called me one morning and said, "I am coming to get you." He was in Punta Gorda, Florida where three giant public schools had been hit by one of the hurricanes. He had been hired by the insurance companies to haul everything to the dump. In order for them to receive their funds, they needed to declare everything a loss. He told me that we could take whatever I wanted. In one particular school, you could hardly even tell anything had happened. In a school for thousands only two classrooms were damaged. Other than that, they were completely intact classrooms. We took down tractor trailers and trucks and we spent fifteen hours with FCS families filling up the trucks with school supplies. We got so much that to this day, eight years later, we have a storage unit and a tractor trailer full of school supplies. We even have a full library in storage if we eventually get a building in which to set it up. We got manipulatives that private schools don't normally have because they cant afford them. And we got them for free. A dye cut machine worth $4,000 was free. We got a whole chemistry lab set up for classrooms. We got paper, folders, globes, boards, tables, literally tens of thousands of dollars worth of materials.

It is clear that God has had His hand in this from the beginning. We cannot afford the teachers we have. I have teachers with masters degrees and from major universities. I have top-notch facilities and supplies. Only God can afford these things.

Our primary goal is to get our kids to have a relationship with Jesus. I really feel like a missionary more than anything else. Honestly, we are not here about education, we're just not. We are not here for reading, math, and science. We are going to be absolutely excellent at education because we have to be to get students to come, but more than anything, we want to tell them about Jesus. We just dressed it like a school.

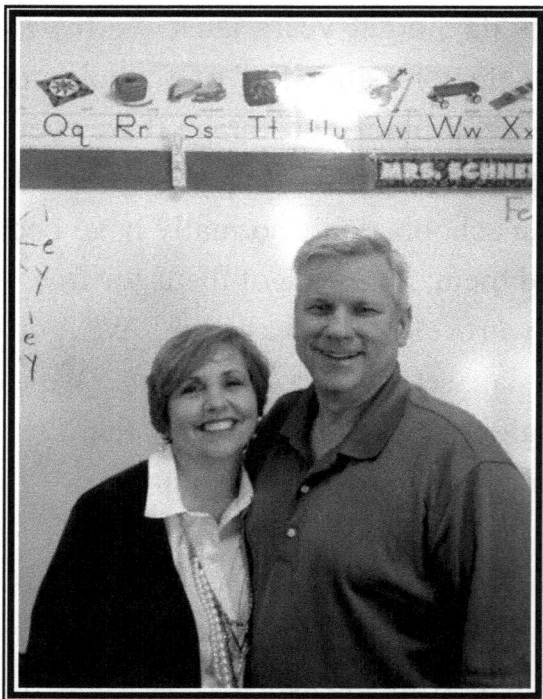

The heart of our school is to disciple children. At times people have come onto our campus and say they can feel the Holy Spirit here. As long as the Holy Spirit is at home here, we know we are doing our jobs.

As told by Terri Schneberger
Winter Garden, Florida

Beauty For Ashes

*To appoint unto them that mourn in Zion, to give unto
them beauty for ashes, the oil of joy for mourning, the
garment of praise for the spirit of heaviness;*

Isaiah 61:3

My story begins with thanksgiving for all that the
Lord has done. He took the wretched life I once knew
and turned it into something beautiful. He has taken
"the years that the cankerworm and wormwood stole"
and restored my life into what He intended from the
beginning. He can do the same for you. I promise.

My childhood up to the age of four was like any
normal childhood. Then we moved to a farm sixty
miles away from both my parents' families and my
world took a turn which brought life-altering events
that would later cause me to make some harmful
decisions. It all began with what I thought was
childhood curiosity, but as the years went by and the
sexual abuse continued, I realized this was not just

35

curiosity but molestation. The perpetrator of this abuse was a good five years older than me. It was revealed to me later in life that he had been sexually abused as a child. Nevertheless, I never felt safe after the first incident. It became a regular thing until I reached sixteen when he finally married. During most of my growing up years I was without the protection I needed and it deprived me of my innocence. Even so, the Lord is faithful and He had a destiny for me.

At the age of nineteen I got married way too young and after four years, we divorced. I later married my high school sweetheart and found myself in a terrible situation. Disturbingly, he turned out to be a wife abuser and an adulterer. I had come to the end of myself and knew I needed an answer. I can't tell you how devastating the shame can be and the fear that enters in when any type of abuse exists.

I was at work one day when I received a call from my cousin. She told me she had become a Christian and wanted me to come for a visit so I could go to church with her. At the time I thought anyone who went to church was a Christian, but she sounded different. So I drove to her home in Oxnard, California and was greeted by an entirely different cousin than I had known growing up. She had always been the tough, party girl, but I could see something had dramatically changed in her life. She had a peace I had never seen in her before. She shared with me how she had received Christ and how much the Lord had done in her life. As I listened with hunger, I realized I was beginning to see a possible solution to my own wrecked life.

We drove over forty miles to attend her church that day. All I remember about the message was that it was mentioned John 3 where Jesus was talking to Nicodemus about being "born again." I didn't receive Christ then, but when I went home, in the privacy of my bedroom, I invited Him into my life. I let go of control. I saw how I had put myself on the throne of my life and I needed Jesus as my Savior. So I prayed and asked Him to become my Lord. I didn't feel anything that night, but the next morning it was as if a "black cloud" had been lifted off my life. Everything was new, bright and beautiful!

I began to see things entirely differently. I had a hunger for His Word and understood it for the very first time. Most importantly, I felt so loved!

Two weeks later I noticed a bible on the receptionist's desk at work and she invited me to a bible study. I immediately got involved in a weekly study at her church and I have never stopped growing in love with Jesus since that day. He has healed me of the rejection, the inferiority, the fear and shame of childhood and adult abuse. In addition, He has empowered me to forgive those who caused the damage. Jesus makes all things new. He will do the same for you no matter what has taken place in your life. He loves you and has such a wonderful plan for your life. He is the answer to whatever you may be facing.

Crystal Koch
Asheville, North Carolina

Qualified by Grace

I was introduced to the message of Grace in the summer of 2000. It was very difficult for me to accept the truth of this message because it was a direct contradiction to everything I knew about God.

This message has many names and I have become acquainted with them all: The Gospel of Peace, True Gospel, Unconditional Love of God, Unconditional Favor of God, God Without Religion, The Gospel of Non-Performance, and many others.

I did not accept this message willingly. In fact, it took almost two full years of intense debate with a grace-filled man whose patience and perseverance I will be forever grateful for.

I have hundreds of fond memories that all involve this new perspective of a God who loves me in spite of my performance; instead of for my performance. My wife and I have had miracles of physical healings, financial breakthroughs, salvations and bondages broken that have all come after this beautiful revelation. By far, the most incredible testimony I have, and probably the foundation for the miracles, healings, provisions, salvations and bondages broken is the sheer magnitude of the freedom that comes with the understanding of a God who isn't as interested in my deeds as He is in me.

I have spent my life (I will be 60 on my next birthday) trying to qualify for God's blessings. I learned this technique from the various churches that I have been acquainted with throughout my life. Grace turns this dynamic upside down. By definition, Grace itself is now my qualifier. Where I always saw a promise with a condition attached to it, I now see every promise as a gift that's already been given, that I only have to accept. After all, what amount of good behavior, or perfection is enough to make you qualified for something God gives? Am I ever qualified? Yes, yes, yes! But only because I'm a son. If I've ever earned it, then it's not free.

This may not sound like much, but when you have spent your life trying to attain something that you never attain, only to finally attain it, but with almost no effort, well, that becomes freeing! I say almost no effort because the only effort needed is to believe that this good news is true! Believing this message leads to ALL the fulfillment of Galatians 5.1: "It was for freedom that Christ set us free."

Joel Mizell
Lakeland, Florida

Beyond Our Wildest Dreams

I was born into a family that most would envy. I was wanted, loved, protected, and provided for. I was raised in church and remember grannies rocking me in the nursery. Churchgoing teetotalers, my parents were called by all "the salt of the earth." Mom, who could sing hymns from memory, was a petite southern belle from a tobacco farm. Dad was a bareback riding, poor Texas storyteller who was an unschooled didactic and mechanical genius.

However, all the church going was no substitute for actually walking with Jesus Christ. Ritual didn't translate into a realization of my true relationship with Him. Hymns and dressing up on Easter Sundays were not Him in a state of grace resurrection in my day to day life. My daily walk was much like being in a garden with a maze of hedges. I believed God had created it, but merely set creation in motion and left it to play itself out. He was the sun shining down from afar, while I wandered aimlessly in a labyrinth. It was full of others just as lost. From Christian ritual I turned to eastern ritual, following a world famous guru whose clients were famous authors, poets, musicians, and celebrities for whom wealth, fame, and education were insufficient. So we all honed our rituals. Not surprisingly, my life full of religious instruction went no better. Poverty, loss of my children, divorce and bankruptcy followed.

I was pregnant, on welfare, awaiting an IRS ruling, when my fourth child came into the world. At her birth the umbilical cord was wrapped around her neck twice. This strangled off her oxygen and shortened the cord until it was ripping out the afterbirth, causing massive bleeding. By a miracle we lived and she suffered no brain damage. After her birth, I went to a spirit-filled Christian church that told of a direct relationship with God that was full of power. They spoke of a born-again (under your spiritual father) life that would conquer all by His power being applied to problems. I attended, took my newborn, and saw my other children baptized there. When my youngest was six, we attended a prayer group led by a woman who opened the group in a different way. She told us to wait on the Holy Spirit. We did not move or speak for over thirty minutes as she had said it may take awhile for our minds to calm down and stop trying to command things. There was no praying or supplication, just watching for God to move.

On that day I felt the presence of Someone coming to stand between me and my daughter. When I looked, I saw a figure in white, coarsely woven, soft cloth robes that somehow glowed. A great peace and sense of wonder came over me. I thought only I had seen this. Many years later, my daughter asked if I had seen the Lord stand next to her. At this point, I knew He was real, but I did not know how to surrender my life in a practical way. How could I let go of the reins and let Him rule my life?

I became a successful sales person, remarried, reconnected with my estranged children, and things were going much better for me. Then 9/11 happened and my husband lost his job. So he went to school to become a chef. We had just built our dream house and were now unsure of how we would pay for it. I was also facing a stressful and unfair situation at work and prayed for guidance. Lonely nights of fear would bring the Comforter to rock me to sleep.

During this time I was invited by a friend to attend a home group where an itinerant preacher spoke. He had a different message of freedom, grace and living in heaven while on earth. He spoke of an option in which man no longer had to experience the traditional route of doubt, disease, and death that we are so familiar with. We also began to listen to a radio host who spoke about freedom, following your God-given talents, and being off the worldly grid. These two individuals made a tremendous impact on our lives. As our perspectives changed, our prayers were answered in miraculous ways.

One message I heard gave me direct guidance into a business decision that solved my work issues. At one point, we needed $59,000 which we did not have, for an important investment. We knew God had led us to this decision, and before the 30 days were up, we had to turn down offers from friends and business acquaintances to help because we had the full amount.

In the following years, the Lord gave us more favor and more ideas. We refinanced our home and opened our first solely owned business of a concession trailer. This has been a tremendous adventure, our lives being saved by angels through road hazards, electrical mistakes and other hardships. We even got invited to join the circus! I left the regular working world and began to work full time with my husband. Now we were totally dependent on what the Lord had for us.

Some months would be great and others brought no paycheck, but the walk with the Lord has been beyond our wildest dreams.

So many miracles have since come to pass. I became reunited with my estranged sister who was miraculously healed of terminal stage four cancer. My oldest daughter conceived late in life, overcoming a very high risk delivery to have a healthy child. Another daughter who vowed to never have children, gave her husband a daughter earlier this year. A condition that my doctor said would cripple my hands has been in remission for 29 years. With our home business we see my mother-in-law and can pray together with her almost daily. Each setback in our business has turned into victory. Our youngest daughter now helps nonverbal autistic children to talk. A son-in-law had a pressure cooker blow up in his face, burning his face, hands, and chest. I told him he would heal immediately, awe the doctors and have no scarring...and it all came to pass!

Our God is everywhere. He is only invisible when we look with our eyes and not our heart. He is only silent when we drown Him out. He is only far when we go independent and run from His will. We stick our own hand in the fire against His warnings and then complain that He has burned us, not reflecting that we were not consumed and don't even smell of smoke. If it seems like you are going through hell, don't stop, keep going. It will not consume you and in the end you won't even smell like smoke.

Beverly Hearn
Midland, Texas

Resting and Rollerblading

As a child I was raised in a Baptist church where I was fully involved. These people were not only my friends but my family. As I reached my later teen years, my parents divorced and my family all went their separate ways. Sadly the one place I should have been able to turn to, my church family, didn't lift me up but instead turned their back on me. Because of this, I left the only family I had intact.

Around the same time, I met a girl who invited me to be part of her church group. I could dance, sing, play cards, laugh and have a good time, all at church. These things were not encouraged in the church I grew up in. I felt in my heart that God was okay with me wanting to dance and sing and be happy. Though I did feel accepted in this new church, I knew that particular religion was not for me.

As I left high school and moved out into the world I always thought about a faith in which I was loved and accepted even if I wasn't acting perfectly 24 hours a day. I believed it existed but I didn't find it in a Baptist church, Mormon church, Catholic church, or Methodist church. For a time I gave up. I wasn't sure that God would be loving, forgiving, accepting and encouraging so I resisted Him. I was discouraged and moved as far away from faith as I could get.

Through the years my life seemed to follow patterns that would repeat themselves over and over. I was the ultimate victim, the ultimate control freak. Jealousy was my best friend and I was fiercely independent. In January 2002 my life spun completely out of control. I had pushed every friend away from me. I broke up with my boyfriend. I had broken relationships with my family and I had just lost my job. I was in the pits. I bargained with God a lot those days and I begged him to forgive me if I took my own life, because I just couldn't go on any further feeling so alone. My heart was broken, I had no faith and certainly had no relationships with anyone at that time. I was alone, depressed and angry.

I prayed for a way out! God gave me a door to step through and I did so, reluctantly. I remember someone suggesting I go to counseling. I thought to myself, "How am I going to go to counseling with no job and no money?" I remember screaming, crying and begging God to get me out of this situation. At this point in my life I felt like I was either going to have to take the easy way out or roll up my sleeves and fully surrender and hope I would see God somewhere along the way, but I doubted it. As I found out later, His plan was better. He wanted me to walk through it, seeing Him at every corner.

As I went to counseling, my (Christian) therapist asked me what I was doing with my days now that I was unemployed. I told her I was treating my day as a work day and working 8:00-5:00 looking for work. I remember her saying, "Maybe it's time to break free from that schedule a bit and do something for yourself." I thought, "She must be crazy! How am I going to find work if I'm not looking for a job?" She asked me what I would like to do for fun and I told her that I had always wanted to learn how to rollerblade. She encouraged me to do it and so I did. I met up with a guy who was part of a group and we skated together during the weekends. Since he was also out of work and loved to skate, he was open to teaching me. We talked a lot and I learned that his father was a preacher and that he attended a large church in my area. I knew I was in a vulnerable place at the time and it had always seemed to me that people would come under the "spell" of Christianity while in a vulnerable place. I determined to not fall victim to that, but did inquire about his faith. Even though he wasn't working, he was positive. There was no pushing, no prodding, he just let me ask my questions. As days went on and I continued rollerblading, I would run into people who were also devoted Christians and were even in ministry. "Oh boy," I thought, "God is surrounding me with Jesus freaks!"

After a couple of months of counseling with my Christian counselor (which wasn't a preference I had been looking for), attending Al-Anon which referenced a Higher Power, and then being surrounded by all these Jesus freaks, I asked if I could go to an Easter service with this man. I immediately felt at home at the church. Something tugged at my heart strings and I knew God was changing me. Soon I began attending this church on Wednesday nights, then also on Sundays. I enjoyed what I was learning and I wanted to share it with everyone. As the months moved by, I made so many wonderful friends from church, Al-Anon and through my new career. I sensed myself being filled with the love of the Lord and I decided to get baptized. August 17, 2003 will always stand out in my mind as the day I found true intimacy, true forgiveness, true acceptance and more love than I could ever imagine.

Through the years and with the help of some beautiful friends, I have learned about the enormity of God's grace towards me. God has revealed how much his grace covered me during those vulnerable moments back in 2002 when He gave me permission to "not work" so I could rest and do something I enjoyed. In doing so, He put people and conversations in my life that helped me learn how loving, encouraging, accepting, forgiving and awesome He really is. It was then that I found a job and embarked on a new career.

My life has been forever changed because of Jesus Christ and I continue to grow in my acceptance of God's amazing grace and unconditional love. As I do, I accept new challenges and walk through new circumstances with a rest and trust that comes from knowing He is my friend and that He is for me.

Carol Ward
Apopka, Florida

A Dog From God

A little over four years ago, my son's dog, Harley, got killed. Harley was Rocket's best friend and we were all devastated. In fact, Rocket was so tore up about it, he told me that he didn't think he would ever want another dog. However, God sometimes uses time to heal our broken hearts. So about six weeks after Harley's death, Rocket told me that he had changed his mind, and thought he would like to have another dog. I told him I thought we ought to pray about it before we did anything else. He agreed. His prayer went something like this, "God, you know we live out in the country and sometimes I get lonely. So Lord, I was thinking that I'd like to have another dog. But I don't want just any dog, I want the dog that You have for me. So I'm going to wait on You. Oh, and God, thank You." (I remember that last part clearly.)

That all took place on a Friday night. The next day, my granddaughter was over playing with him in the yard, when all of a sudden she came running through the door and exclaimed, "Meemo, Rocket found a puppy!" I figured it probably belonged to one of our neighbors so I went to see. As I rounded the corner of the house, I saw my son holding this little scraggly, mangy, bag of bones. And she smelled worse than she looked! But there he stood, holding this pitiful little pup up next to his heart and smiling like he had found a great treasure. "Look Mom! Oh look what God gave me! He gave me a puppy just like I asked for!" I said, "Oh Son, does it have to be this puppy?" I'll never forget the look of confusion and disappointment on my son's face at that moment. With his most serious tone, he asked, "How are you gonna do that?" "Do what, Son?" "Ask God for something, and then when He gives it to you, tell Him it's not good enough."

That day, we started the long process of getting her well. I simply did not have the money to take her to the vet, so I got on my computer and typed in all her symptoms, and began every home remedy we could find. Every day Rocket and I laid hands on her, and we prayed. We prayed for healing. We prayed for wisdom. Some days we just prayed for strength! One day I walked in and found her dripping with oil from head to toe. Rocket had anointed her! He said, "I wasn't sure how much to use, so just to be safe I poured the whole thing on her!" I might mention at this point, that "the whole thing" he was referring to, was a $65 bottle of olive oil, which incidentally, was sitting in the cabinet right beside a cheap bottle of olive oil.

We had tried everything, but she just wasn't getting any better. So, once more we prayed, and I called the vet. I'll never forget the conversation I had that day with the lady that answered the phone. I explained the whole situation to her, including the part where I didn't have any money. She said that because Noel (that's what he named her) was basically a "rescue" to go ahead and bring her in and they'd let me pay it out. Wow God! And so it began...she started the long journey that would lead to happy and healthy.

One day, I asked Rocket if he'd ever thanked God for Noel, and he assured me that he had. "Did you?" he asked. "Well, yes Son, I did." "Oh, I didn't know that you knew," he said. "Knew what?" I asked. "That she was worth saving." I stood there that day, broken...broken before my God and my son...knowing full well that that's what God sees when He looks at us. Even when we're at our worst, He sees something "worth saving."

It took us about two years to get Noel completely well. One day I made a remark to Rocket about how "pretty" she is now. He said, "What do you mean 'now'?" And once again I was reminded of how God sees us. Rocket had never seen what I saw the first time I laid eyes on this pup that God had used to teach me so much. All he had ever seen was the beautiful gift that God had given him.

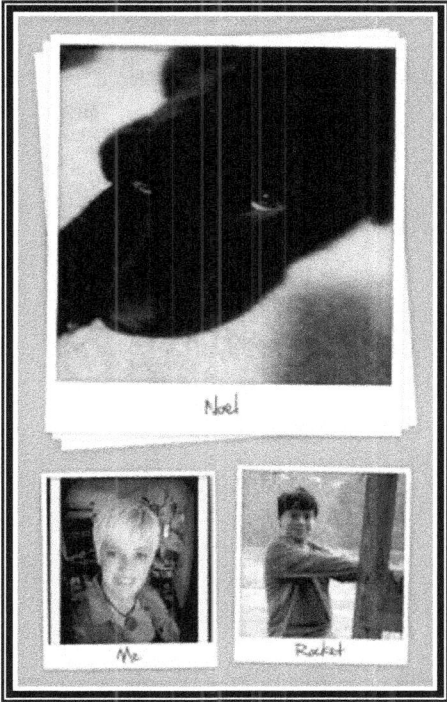

Noel

Me   Rocket

Now, as you've probably guessed, Noel has turned out to be the best dog we've ever had. And it's not uncommon for people to mention how impressed they are that she is so good-natured, well behaved, and obedient.

The other day, I overheard one of Rocket's friends talking about how "good" she is. He asked, "Where did you get her anyway?" I smiled as I heard my son give the answer that I knew he would give: "God gave her to me."

Bren Claborn
Author of "Love God, Love People, Love Like Jesus"
Mena, Arkansas

Walking Out of Depression

Seven years ago, I sunk into a deep depression. I had been depressed before, but not for the past ten years since I had become a Christian. I had thought that kind of despair was in my past. In fact, it was my testimony – God had released me from a hauntingly self-destructive past and had delivered me into a new and hopeful life. Yet somehow I had found myself extremely disappointed with life, with God and particularly with my circumstances. A serious relationship was ending, I had lost my job, I was uninspired creatively. I had damaged other significant relationships with choices I had made. My heart was at a loss at the seemingly utter failure of my life. Most days I could barely get out of bed and some days I wouldn't. I wouldn't shower. I canceled get togethers with friends because I felt so needy and unlovable and frankly, I did not want them to see me like that. I gained weight. I would sleep for 12-14 hours at a stretch. Enjoyment of anything was a thing of the past.

I did not go down easily. I tried everything I knew to not accept this depression. I memorized scriptures that addressed depression, I sang praise songs even when I did not feel the least like singing. I read my bible. I went to church and tried to get involved even though I felt a million miles away from people. It all felt phony and empty and dead. I saw a therapist (in fact I had spent nearly half my life in therapy, both Christian and secular). I was prescribed three different anti-depression medicines by a Harvard educated Christian psychiatrist. At times, I imagined Christian friends judging me because of a belief that real Christians cannot get depressed. But honestly, the revulsion I felt towards myself in this state made me willing to try anything to get myself out of this awful hell.

I remember I would drive to work in the morning and all my thoughts would be shaming thoughts: thoughts of what I had done wrong in the relationship that ended, thoughts of the people I had hurt or mistakes I had made, thoughts of being alone for life, thoughts of how I grew up believing I was unlovable, and that maybe deep down I was scarred and really could not change. Several times a day, at my new office job, I would burst into tears and hope that no one would notice. I would go over and over these awful memories and thoughts in my head in the desperate hope of somehow fixing things. But all it did was reinforce that I was a hopeless case. I found myself languishing in the midst of this awful quagmire (and if you've ever been depressed, you know that it is very much like being stuck in quicksand). You are smarter than this. You know better. You don't want to be there. Yet you remain and sometimes you even think it would be better to end it all just to escape the self-disgust and pain.

One day I was on the internet and I was reading an excerpt from a Christian book about gaining victory over depression. The author stated that all depression stems from wrong thinking. And if your thinking gets corrected, your feelings will follow your thoughts. I remember it offended me. Didn't he think I was smart enough to know wrong thinking and correct it? I knew I was helpless because I had tried everything. I decided it was just one of those low budget "Christianese-type" books written by someone with no experience in the real world.

Yet those words stayed with me over the following months and I inadvertently and gradually began to do just that. One of the main things I began to consider was that God deeply and unconditionally loved me. Please understand, I had always said that God loved me, but it was a wavering sort of love. I saw Him like most humans – He loved me when I was good and distanced Himself or punished me when I was not. His love was dependent on my actions and words. However, now when I found myself unconsciously reliving mistakes I had made, I would stop and firmly say to myself, "No. God delights in me. He thinks I am lovely and worthwhile...even though I have made serious mistakes." Proverbs 23:7 says, As a man thinks in his heart, so is he. I purposed to believe that what God said about me would trump what I or others believed about me. It was a slow, steady, retraining of my thinking and it was based on the Truth found in the Bible. I began to see scripture in a new light and perspective. My eyes were opened to a vast, unconditional, unchanging, nurturing love that I had never fully seen in all my years of bible study. I immersed myself in teaching that focused on the love and grace of God and I began to see changes and healing in my thinking.

There had always been a sort of desperate element to my relationship with God. I was always seeking and searching to be closer to Him, to love Him better, to do better. But now I felt God instructing me to rest, to relax, and to receive from Him. I began to realize that I had had it backwards. I had been trying to prove my love for Him by doing things for Him. Instead, I realized that as a Christian, I was joined to Him and therefore a new creation in Him. I couldn't get any closer to Him than that. Resting took me out of my performance mindset and put everything onto a loving God. Quite honestly, this did not come easily or naturally to me. I was afraid that if I let go of "working" and "pushing" that I would end up on my couch living a life of apathy. It was counter-intuitive, but it did produce results. Surprisingly, opportunities to love and bless others arose naturally and were more effective and lasting when flowing out of my rest in His unconditional love.

I discovered that God was not against me, but that sin has its own natural consequences. My suffering and disappointment with my life were not a result of His frustration with me. In fact, receiving God's love and grace enabled me to make better choices. When I felt secure in His love for me, I had a confidence and sturdiness that enabled me to overcome addictions and temptations that I had never been able to overcome when I was trying to do it in my own strength.

Another important thing I learned was that mixture of the Old Covenant and the New Covenant produced confusion. The Old Covenant was an agreement between God and the Jewish nation and was full of types and shadows that all pointed to Jesus. The New Covenant was between God and all people, Jew or Gentile and offered something so much better than the Old it was literally called the Good News! Jesus did not abolish the Old Covenant, but He did fulfill it. The New Covenant offers forgiveness of all our sins (past, present and future), union with the Creator of the Universe, and access to the Kingdom of God here and now.

It took some time for these truths and others like them to take root and have a real impact on my thinking and the living of my life. I thought I knew a lot about the bible and about psychology and recovery, but facing something like depression revealed what I really believed deep down. Intellectual assent is not the same thing as having an experience. I am thankful to say that because of this walk out of depression, my faith is more authentic and more enjoyable than it ever has been. My faith is not in a doctrine. It is in the person of Jesus Christ.

I don't look for formulas anymore and I won't offer any to those of you who may be navigating depression, disappointment or discouragement. I will not enter debates about medication or therapy or the suggestion that true Christians can't become depressed. We are all growing. I will tell you that I have lived without depression, medication or therapy for over three years now. I do not believe it will return, but even if it did, I know the Lord can and will walk me through it. In the meantime, I am thrilled to be experiencing true enjoyment of life. I am seeing heaven everywhere. If you are dealing with anything like I did, I have hope for you. You may not follow the same path I did (in fact, I hope you do better), but a revelation of God's unconditional love is always available for you.

Judi Manis
Winter Garden, Florida

Still Blessed

At the young age of ten, I was saved and baptized. When I was fourteen, I was baptized in the Holy Ghost. There have been many pot holes along the way, some mountains to climb and valleys to walk through, but God always walked with me in the rough places. He always brought me to victory. God gave me a song called "Leading Me" that I recorded on one of my CD's.

By the grace and mercy of God, I don't have a testimony about how God delivered me from a lot of bad things. I was raised in a godly home with wonderful parents and I lived a very sheltered life. My grandfather was a minister of the gospel. God blessed me with a talent to play the piano and sing. I traveled with my grandfather and played and sang while he ministered. He made a great impression on my life. I was an only child until I was ten years old. I was then blessed with a sister and a brother. I was always very God-conscious as a child.

I graduated from high school at the age of sixteen and I went straight to San Antonio International Bible College. I came back home and married my childhood sweetheart at the age of seventeen. He worked for an oil company and we were transferred from one place to another. I attended many churches and I heard many things, some of which I had to take Paul's words to Timothy. 2 Timothy 2:15 says, *Study to show thyself approved unto God, a workman that needeth not to be ashamed, rightly dividing the word of truth.* I still try to take those same words of advice. The Word becomes more precious to me daily as I read it and I realize who I am in Christ and the benefits I have in being His child. He told us not to forget all of His benefits. Proverbs 30:5 says, *Every word of God is Pure. He is a shield unto them that put their trust in Him.*

The roughest valley I ever walked through was when my husband died after forty-three years of marriage. We were blessed with three wonderful children, one daughter and two sons. They and their families are all devout Christians. They have been a real strength to me through everything.

God took care of me through all the changes. A man operating five nursing facilities called to see if I would go to work for him traveling from one facility to the other entertaining as an activity director. He paid for my schooling while I worked. It has been a wonderful experience meeting and ministering to so many people and singing for them. I feel God placed me right where I needed to be. I am 84 years of age and I still work two or more days a week. God has been so faithful and good to me. I believe in asking big of God, because He has an abundant supply of whatever we need.

One of the highlights of my life was in 1992 when I went to Russia (Ukraine) as a missionary for three weeks. I got to meet people who were anxious to hear about Jesus and I was happy to tell them.

My journey of life has been great and it gets sweeter every day. I believe in enjoying where we are until we get to where we are going.

Geneva Norwood
Cunningham, Texas

Grace in Healing

Life was good and I knew I was blessed the years before the illness and events that nearly took my life. My family and I had been living in Florida for eight years after relocating from Illinois where most of our family resides. My husband, Doug, was growing in his career while mine was ending after 23 years in healthcare management. I had begun an exciting acting and modeling career which I loved and was enjoying moderate success in the local industry. Most of all, I was enjoying the time I spent homeschooling my youngest son, watching my beautiful family blossom with marriages for my two oldest and grandchildren arriving exponentially. We loved our church, our community, our friends, and the ministry I was in (teaching a women's bible study). I never once doubted the blessings of God or took for granted the riches in our life that came from Him.

Then my health began to change. I began having some bothersome symptoms that seemed to not go away. Rashes, itching, and pain were the mysterious symptoms that none of the doctors could seem to explain. After a few months, my mother suggested that I look into testing to see if the problems could be related to the silicone breast implants that I'd had for 24 years. By that time, I was seeing a rheumatologist who was becoming more worried that I had a very serious and rare autoimmune disease. I could not even say the name or acknowledge it. God knew I had a problem with "labels" including those that came in the form of a diagnosis – not just for me, but for anybody. My philosophy was rooted in my belief that only God could define us, and I was beginning to understand who I was in Jesus Christ.

One day as I was quietly taking a relaxing bath, I said to the Lord, "God, I don't know what's going on inside this body, but you do. I am scared, but I will trust you in all things. I appoint you my Primary Care Physician, my Healer, my Comforter. Help me and guide me as I seek medical care." During the months to follow, I found out that the implants had disintegrated inside my body requiring them to be removed. I felt alone because most of my doctors would not even acknowledge that there might be a correlation between the toxicity in my body and the autoimmune disease, therefore, I was getting very little direction. I knew that the Lord was directing me to pursue removing the poison both medically and naturally. I know had I not pursued the surgeries, I would not be here today. The morning of my second surgery after I had been meditating and clinging to the words of Psalm 91, I looked down and saw that the shirt I chose to wear was my husband's which had two spans of feathered wings across my chest. The words from the fourth verse, He will cover you with his feathers, and under his wings you will find refuge; his faithfulness will be your shield and rampart came quickly to mind, and I knew I would be okay.

Then came the diagnosis of scleroderma. With the form and aggression that I had came a prognosis that had the potential to end my life, especially if there was internal involvement. Thankfully, there was no evidence of this. I began to deteriorate rapidly as my body began to change and my hands became debilitated. As I sought treatment and support from my wonderful family who never stopped praying for me or believing for my healing, I began to question just what the Word said about healing. After all, I had prayed for others countless times and had the faith to believe for their healing, but I was not so sure about mine. I had incredible pain like nothing I had experienced before and infections with which there was an ongoing battle. Long-suffering was the only way I could describe it. My wonderful mother, Rose, moved in with us to help care for me when I could no longer dress myself, tend to my ulcers, and take care of my family, including a daughter battling addiction, and a few grandchildren. We had by then made another life transition when we moved to upstate New York for my husband's job. We were now alone, away from our church and family and friends, and going through very difficult and dark times. This was becoming more than I could bear, or anyone else in our household could bear as well.

But God was there. And so was His Word. In fact, it never left me. I knew that the grace teaching we had received under my pastor and the prayers of the saints, especially from his sweet and compassionate wife, as well as my beloved family and friends, were deeply implanted in me. God had poured into me the revelation of the finished work of Christ, which included the healing already done for me (and you). He reminded me of my identity in Him, and that the very root issue of the disease that afflicted me was "rejection of self," and that was not how He sees me. I must continue to walk in the acceptance that is for me and of me. At times when life was so overwhelming, I would recall the Good News of God's grace and healing that were mine. Prayers and words of encouragement were brought to mind and always in a timely manner. Joy would always overshadow the grief of physical loss.

I was very thankful for the Lord's provision with a dedicated husband who never saw me as anything less than the beautiful wife he married, grandchildren who would pray for me and bring their healing touch by helping me in so many ways, the finances to pay for the best healthcare, a beautiful home, and family who surrounded me. Yes, it was stressful and chaotic at times, but we learned to trust in God's faithfulness and rest in His presence. I began to walk in a new expectation, that even though my circumstances were difficult beyond the comprehension or the experience of most, I did not lose hope that I would continue to get better and that healing would be seen through me and in me.

We have since happily returned home to Florida. I've learned that sometimes despite what we see or feel, the truth of God's kingdom far outweighs the facts of this world. Most of all, despite dealing with physical afflictions, I have received the goodness of grace and can still say, "Life is good, because God is good."

Katie Roof
Oviedo, Florida

A Modern Day Miracle

Last September we sold our home in Las Vegas. We were packed and ready to drive to Texas where we now live. We rented a u-haul trailer to pull our belongings back with us. My husband, Jessie, had recently undergone neck surgery and was wearing a neck brace so I would have to drive. We were more than ready to get back home so I asked him, "The speed limit says to go 55, what do you think?" He said, "Oh, you can probably go 60-65." So I maneuvered our Chevy Avalanche truck pulling the trailer onto I95, which is a five lane highway. It was a Friday morning about 8:00. I accelerated to 65 and got into the middle lane when the trailer began to fishtail. It surprised me and I could not get it to stop fishtailing by adjusting the steering. I asked the Lord, "What do I do?" I heard, "STOP!" I stomped on the brake and we stopped. Miraculously, we stopped and no one hit us. In fact, no one was hurt.

I said to Jessie, "What do I do now?" He said, "Turn to the left." I was facing the center cement wall separating us from the oncoming traffic and in the center lane. I turned left which made the sun behind me. As I turned, I saw a bright white light and the five lanes of traffic were stopped in a semicircle. All the time I kept saying, "Thank you Lord! Thank you Lord! Thank you Lord!

We got out to ascertain the damage and there were two holes in the back bumper, a dent on the left back fender and the trailer brake lost the rubber gasket off of it. The u-haul place called a mobile repairman to fix it and we were on our way.

That evening we stopped in Flagstaff, Arizona for the night. I could not go to sleep because I kept going over and over the near accident in my mind. Finally, at 3:00am I prayed, "Lord, please show me what I need to learn here because I need to rest and sleep so I will be able to drive again in the morning." I got up and began writing on the La Quinta notepad. This is what God gave me:

My Darling, I am your shepherd.
I will not lead you down a path that I cannot keep you.
Look up and see the light that leads to all truth.
Fear not my little flock for I am with you.

For I calm the sea; I calm the wind.
I calm you as you hear my voice and see the light on
your path.
You are safe in me.
For I am your God and there is NO thing stronger or
mightier than me.
I calmed the traffic.
I turned you around.
I caused you to see my hand and way.
Go forward NOW!

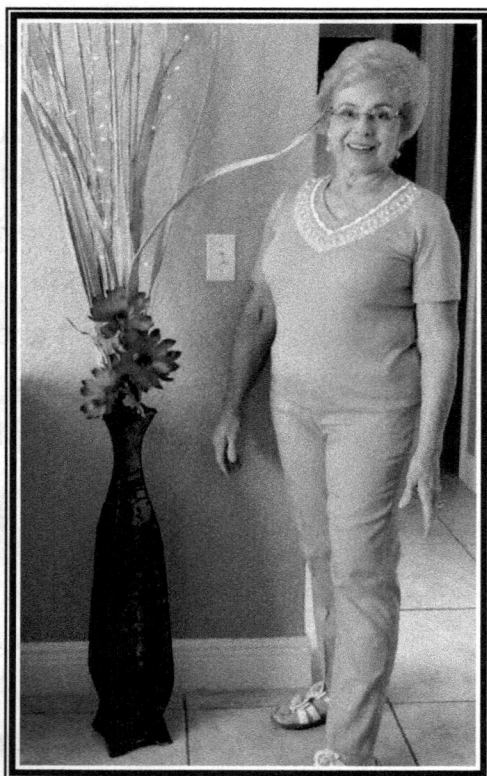

I went back to bed and slept soundly What an awesome God we have living within us and yet has the power over all He has created in this world, for as He said that night, "There is NO thing stronger or mightier than God."

Dianne Price
Midland, Texas

A Fresh Perspective

I had been involved with a local church for a couple years. Within a short time of joining this church, which was pastored by a longtime friend of mine, I took over the youth ministry. I served as the youth leader for over a year. During this time I grew spiritually and saw the youth grow immensely. I saw manifestations of healing, I saw the grace and love of God move mightily and change the lives of the youth and those I served along with at the church.

I preached my heart out. I was sold out for Christ. I grew in the Word and I stood on the Word when attacks came. During a time when I was teaching on health and healing, an attack came on my unborn son. The doctors tried to tell us that there was a very strong possibility that he would have Down syndrome. I laughed when I heard the news. I thought, "Of course; well played devil," because what greater way to discredit my teaching than to bring something like this on my family. My wife and I prayed and took our authority through the finished work of Christ over the situation. Nevertheless, as hard as we can pray, and as well as we can articulate our declarations and proclamations of the Word, without love, we're still behind the eight ball. After all, faith works by love. (Galatians 5:6)

Thankfully, my wife and I were at a point in our walk where we had this revelation of love. We are human and we love our unborn son, yet God is greater. If we wanted to see our child whole, how much more would our heavenly Father want to see him whole? (Matthew 7:11) How could we honestly say that we love our child more than God does? The end result?

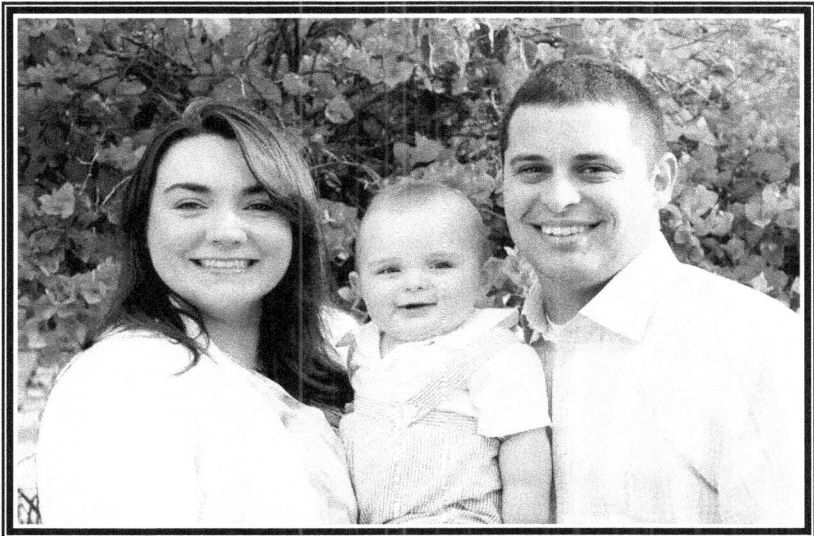

I may be partial, but he is the sweetest and most beautiful child you could ever meet, and he is completely whole in every way. To God be the glory! I tell you that to illustrate this: I knew the Word, I operated in its principles, and I had a revelation of the love and grace of God. Without this revelation, I have no doubt my son's outcome would've been different.

Time went by and the pastors at my church wanted to try something different from the normal youth ministry model. At the time God was leading me to do something else in the church, so it was perfect timing and so I transitioned into my new role. During this time a relationship with one our fellow church leaders was shattered and my family and I prayed about what to do. We felt it was time to go elsewhere. So we did.

This relationship was more than just a normal ministry relationship. We were like family and very close. The things that happened boggled my mind and really hurt me as well as my family. The cut was deep, but I was determined to not let it hinder my love walk or allow strife and bitterness to form in my heart.

For a long time I've held the belief that feelings can lie. If I have a feeling that does not line up with what my Spirit has (love, joy, peace, etc), I simply rebuke it. So this is how I tried to handle the hurt feelings I had. I loved this person, and tried to extend grace and not walk in bitterness, but it was a constant struggle. I often wondered how long this battle would go on. I was attempting to extend grace, love, and mercy, but I was doing it in my own power.

Roughly six months later I ended up running into my old friend while I was attending a conference with my new church. I was believing for a restoration of friendship, but sadly the encounter was not what I had hoped for. However, something started happening. As I walked back to the hotel with two of my friends, I inadvertently spoke out what I had for so long denied, "What happened hurt me, and it feels like a knife in my heart!" As soon as I spoke those words my mind went on the fritz. I walked into my hotel room and the tears I had held in for so long began to flow.

Sitting in my room, I quietly listened as God ministered to me personally. For so long I had been denying the existence of this wound. For so long I had denied that there was anything that needed to be fixed. The problem was that I was not addressing the root cause of why I was having these feelings. By rejecting the feelings of hurt and betrayal, I was denying that anything was wrong.

I began to realize that in denying this wound's existence, I had not given God the chance to work in my life. How could I allow the love of God to restore me if I denied that there was ever a problem with me to begin with? How could I make Jesus the Lord of my life in an area that had been damaged if I denied that there was anything to be Lord over? How could I lay something at the altar, if I denied its very existence?

At that moment I realized I was trying so hard to do something supernatural without the One who is supernatural. When I addressed the problem in this manner, there was a release. No longer was I battling against these emotions or thoughts. I was allowing God's love and grace to heal what had been damaged and to bring me to a place of perfect peace. It felt so amazing that I searched my heart for other areas that I had been holding onto and addressed them as well. The result was freedom, peace, a fullness of joy, and pure love.

I walked out of my hotel the next morning with a spring in my step and a newfound revelation of God's love and grace that re-energized my soul. Though I knew the Word and saw breakthroughs in other areas of my life, in this particular situation, I needed a fresh perspective. Once I let God in and His grace and love do it's work, it was finished...

Charlie Lombard
Titusville, Florida

I'm Always With You

I am a marketer for a home health agency. One of our offices was having some problems with their census, so our company decided to have a marketing blitz in that area. They sent all marketers to this one office, and our job was to saturate the surrounding areas with brochures, cards, pens, and notepads – anything and everything to get our name out.

I arrived at the office and they gave me a paper with the three locations that I was to market that day. My supervisors handed me a box with loads of information and marketing tools for the places I would be. I had no clue where these three towns were, much less where I would need to go to find potential patients. I was a little anxious, to say the least, about heading out for a whole day without a plan at all. I realized that I had driven my little work car that day which did not have a navigation system, so all I had was my trusty side kick, my cell phone.

As I got in my car, I turned on my worship music and headed in the direction that I was to go. I was singing and praying, and I asked God to guide me to where I needed to be and to lead me to the people I needed to talk to as well as the places I needed to go. I drove about thirty miles and came upon the first location. I found myself in a small town square that had a few simple shops, a couple barbershops and some other small offices. I went ahead and pulled in and parked.

At first I thought I would check my cell phone and see if there was a hospital or a doctor's office nearby to visit, but as I sat in my car, I saw a little old man walk into a barbershop. I decided to just walk around and hand out brochures in the town square. I walked into a few of the store fronts and gave out my information. I headed across the street to a couple more and a woman standing in front of the finance store asked me, "Can I help you?" I explained to her that I was marketing for a home health company and asked if I could give her some brochures. She looked at the brochure and said, "I need to talk to you right now." She took me into her finance office and proceeded to tell me that she had two elderly ladies living with her and both needed home health. She gave me information that she should never even have known. There were insurance cards, social security numbers, birthdays to the year and all their medical needs. I was floored. I would have never gone into that finance office. That's not somewhere potential patients would normally be.

I got back into my car and called the office. I had only been gone for forty-five minutes and it took me thirty minutes to even get to the town. I told them that I had two possible referrals and I had all their information. They could not believe it!

I covered the rest of the town with a smile that went from ear to ear. I made some stops at a couple nursing homes, assisted living facilities, and other places. I headed to the second town and then the third.

The third town was almost just as small as the first. It had a dollar store and a hardware store. I was very surprised to see that it did have a doctor's office and I was able to leave some things with them. As I got back into my car I saw a huge Ford truck pull into an office building across the parking lot. When the man got out, I noticed that he looked really familiar. Then I just happened to glance up at the rear view mirror and saw a banner with a woman's picture on it. She, too, looked very familiar. Suddenly I realized that she was a woman who attends our church some sixty miles away. I had no idea that she had an office in this small town. In fact, I did not even know that she was a nurse practitioner. I tried the office door, but it was locked, so I called the number on the banner. "What time do you open back up from lunch?" I asked. She said, "Are you in the parking lot?" "Yes, ma'am," I replied. She said,"Come on in, I'll open the door for you."

I explained to her that I went to church with the doctor and wanted to give her a few things. A couple of minutes later, the doctor and her husband came out. She said, "Well, we knew an Amber, but wondered what in the world is she doing all the way over here?" I gave her the whole story of our marketing plan, and what I was doing in their area. She made my day even better by telling me that she had a successful practice with tons of patients that a home health agency loves to get. We had a great little talk and I returned to my car to head home.

As I got into my car, my smile was now even bigger. I was in awe of how great our God is. As I cried, still in shock of His guidance throughout the day, He quietly spoke to me, "I'm always with you. You just have to stop and listen." As a busy mom, marketer and the one who takes care of our cattle, it was such an eye opener for me. He reminded me to take a minute and enjoy the goodness that He has me and for each of us. 'Cause He is so GOOD!!!

Amber Galloway
Cunningham, Texas

www.ingramcontent.com/pod-product-compliance
Lightning Source LLC
Chambersburg PA
CBHW060034050426
42448CB00012B/3004